PLANTERS PEANUT™

Since 1961

COLLECTIBLES

A Handbook and Price Guide

Jan Lindenberger
with Joyce Spontak

77 Lower Valley Road, Atglen, PA 19310

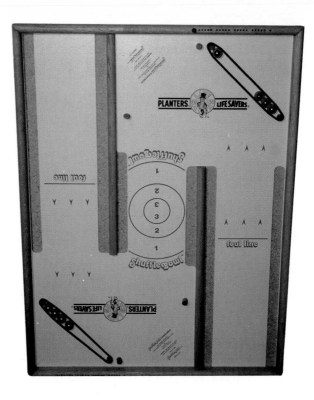

Library of Congress Cataloging-in-Publication Data

Lindenberger, Jan.
    Planters Peanut collectibles since 1961: a handbook and price guide/Jan Lindenberger with Joyce Spontak.
       p. cm.
    ISBN 0-88740-793-5 (paper)
    1. Planters Peanuts (Firm)--Collectibles--Catalogs. I. Spontak, Joyce. II. Title.
NK808.L57   1995
338.7'6648056595--dc20   95-31083
                                        CIP

Printed in Hong Kong.
ISBN: 0-88740-793-5

Published by Schiffer Publishing, Ltd.
77 Lower Valley Road
Atglen, PA 19310
Please write for a free catalog.
This book may be purchased from the publisher.
Please include $2.95 postage.
Try your bookstore first.

We are interested in hearing from authors with book ideas on related topics.

Contents

Acknowledgments

Many thanks to Joyce and Robert Spontak. These wonderful people opened up their home and allowed me to photograph their extensive and varied collection. The majority of the information for this book came from these well-informed people. Joyce was once an employee of the Planters Peanut Company.

I really appreciated her patience and the hours of arranging and rearranging her wonderful collection. Especially since it was through the Christmas holidays.

Joyce and Bob have been collecting Mr. Peanut and Planters items for many years. It all started when Joyce's grandmother gave her a plastic bank in the shape of Mr. Peanut. Years later, as an adult, she found a matching cup and then a mechanical pencil. When her husband gave her a large store six-sided jar, she believed she then had every item Planters ever made.

In their active pursuit of Mr. Peanut items, they found out about and joined Peanut Pals, a group of collectors who shared their interests. Since that time their collection has grown considerably. Joyce became editor of the club's bi-monthly newsletter for the next six years. If anyone has any questions or needs information on any Planters item they may contact Joyce at (412) 221-7599 or by mail at 804 Hickory Grade Road, Bridgeville, Pennsylvania. 15017.

Also many thanks to Van Benedick. Without his help much of this book would not have been possible. He opened his home and allowed us to photograph his one-of-a-kind collection. Van was also a wonderful source of pricing and dating items.

Further thanks goes to Ed and Arleane Pawlowicz, Marty and Pam Blank, and to anyone else we may have forgotten.

Introduction

In 1889, at age 12, Amedeo Obici arrived in New York from Italy. He had virtually no money and couldn't speak English, yet he was determined to make his own way in this new country. After moving to Wilkes-Barre, Pennsylvania, and a brief bout of formal schooling, he worked at various jobs, including his uncle's fruit stand. In 1896 he bought a peanut roaster and went into business for himself. The rest is history.

In 1913 the Planters Nut and Chocolate Company moved to Suffolk, Virginia, closer to where peanuts were grown, and built its own factory for processing and packaging. Two more plants eventually opened: the San Francisco plant in 1921 and the Toronto, Canada plant in 1925.

In 1961, after 55 years of the family style leadership of a private company, Planters Nut and Chocolate Company was acquired by Standard Brands, a subsidiary of Nabisco Brands. In the years that followed, Nabisco Brands merged with R.J. Reynolds Tobacco Company to form R.J.R. Nabisco. In 1988 three business men, Kravis, Kohlberg and Roberts, exercised a leveraged buy-out to acquire R.J.R. Nabisco. Both the Toronto, Canada and San Francisco plants are now closed and the original Suffolk, Virginia factory was replaced in 1994 with a new, totally modern facility. Except for the Peanut Store in Suffolk, Virginia, all of the peanut stores are either closed or are privately owned.

1918

1919

1920

1922

Through the years Planters has been the leader in the market of nuts. Under each change in ownership, they have also produced a great number of advertising premiums. The "newer" items, though not as valuable as those of the Planters Nut and Chocolate Company years, increase in value each year. Some items, such as the plastic bank and the mechanical pencil, were so popular that they were first made under Planters Nut and Chocolate Company and continued until recently. Even though the items looked the same initially, there is an old version and a new version which are easily distinguishable. Also, Planters sponsored race car and a golf tournament, generating many collectibles. Mr. Peanut turned 75 years old in 1991. The company did a splendid job with birthday premiums during this time.

In recent years, the company has used various logos, some with and some without Mr. Peanut. The PLS-(Planters-Lifesaver) forklift design was not as popular as the Heritage logo where Mr. Peanut stands in front of a large red lifesaver. The Heritage logo was discontinued at the end of 1991. Items without Mr. Peanut do not have the value to collectors that items with Mr. Peanut do.

The items in this book are from 1961 through 1994. The information and pictures shown here are intended to assist in the knowledge of what items were produced, their cost, and authenticity. Prices may vary from those listed due to geographical location and condition of the item. The prices are based on cost averaging-not on an isolated sale and definitely not on price tags on unsold items. A "price not available" notation is necessary on some of these collectibles.

Our first volume, *Planters Peanut Collectibles: 1906-1961*, has many other items plus a chapter on reproductions. This is particularly helpful in light of the many reproduced items on the market.

1926

1923   1925

1948 and into the 1950s

1962 and into the 1980s

1957

1927 to 1945

1990

1991-1994

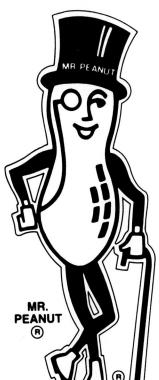

1995 to present

Plastics

Plastic sign. Nut Center. 49". 1980s. Also came in a smaller 33.5" size printed on 2 lines. $25-$40.

Plastic advertising sign with Mr. Peanut logo in the corner. 40". 1990s. $25-35.

Plastic Mr. Peanut banner. 1988. $20-40.

Plastic doll house that has a sign on top that reads "bring Planters home for the holidays". 1989. $50-75.

Plastic head two-piece counter display. Removable hat. 1979. $15-25.

White plastic counter display. 8.5". 1960s-70s. $25-40.,

Clear plastic counter display bowl. 8".
1960s-70s. $30-45.

24 ounce peanut oil in plastic bottles.
1990s. $4-6.

Plexiglass plastic counter top display and dispenser. 1970s. $125-165.

Plastic display rack for peanut products. 1980s. $15-25.

Plastic yellow base peanut butter maker in original box with all attachments. 12.5" tall. Made by Picam, Richard, or Emenee, 1976. $20-45.

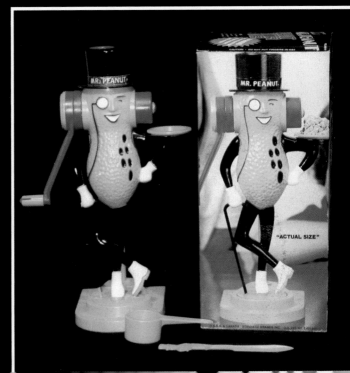

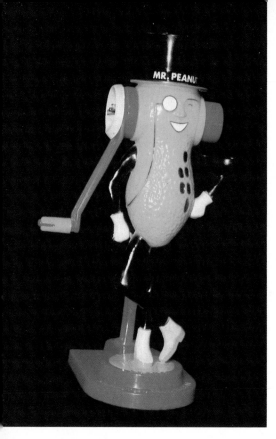

Southern Belle, Planters company nut chopper. 1970. $15-25.

Plastic peanut butter maker by Emenee. Note the rare red base and back pole. Complete with all accessories in box. 1976. $45-75.

Set of four plastic coasters in a clear box. Each has Mr. Peanut on front. 4". 1994. $35-50.

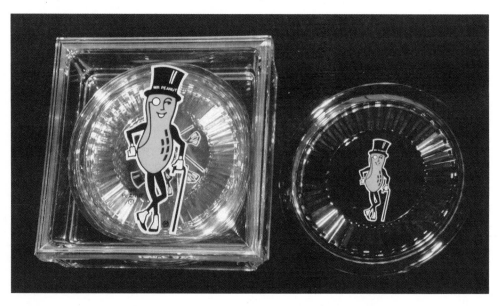

Styrofoam can holder. 1981. $5-8.

Clear plastic one gallon tea container
with Mr. Peanut painted on front. 1980.
$20-30.

Plastic top hat nut dish. 1993. 4" X 7". $8-
12.

Plastic top hat ice bucket. 1992. 8" x 11".
$15-25.

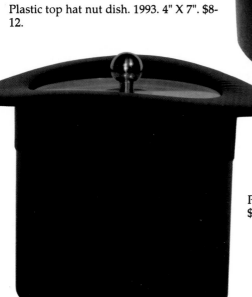

13

Four Plastic tumblers in red, clear, purple, gold. 1970s. 4.5". $20-25 each.

Yellow plastic pitcher and 4 glasses with blue Mr. Peanut. 1970s. $25-40.

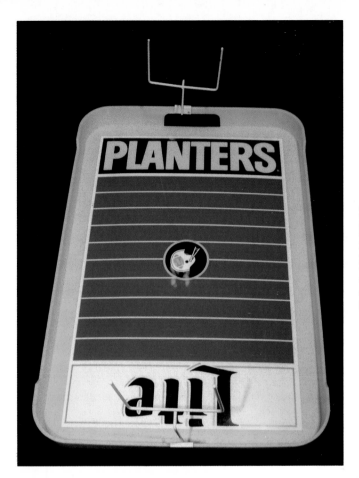

Plastic tray with football field design. Has advertising for Planters and Lite beer in the endzones. Clip-on goal posts for each end. 1984. 13.5" x 20". $15-20.

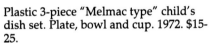

Plastic 3-piece "Melmac type" child's dish set. Plate, bowl and cup. 1972. $15-25.

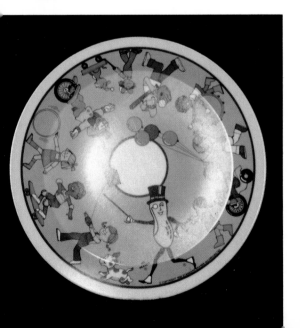

Plastic mug with blue background. 1978.
$7-12.

Plastic insulated tumbler with "Heritage
" logo. 1990. $10-14.

Plastic cup and straw with Heritage
logo. 1989. $10-15.

Insulated travel coffee mug with plastic
holder. Can fit on the car door or stick to
the dash. 1994. $6-10.

Plastic yellow squeeze bottle with straw. 1990. $15-20.

Plastic blue squeeze bottle with red straw from the Ft. Smith, Arkansas plant. 1993. $10-15.

Plastic squeeze drinking bottle with straw. Munch and Go design on yellow bottle front with a running Mr. Peanut. 1993. $5-8.

Blue plastic Thermos-style bottle with strap. 1985. $15-20.

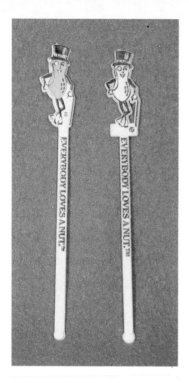

Plastic drink stirrers from promotion.

Enlargement of the plastic stirrers. The first version (left) is black and white with a yellow body and monocle drilled out. 1993. $5-8. The second version (right) is black and white. 1993. $2-3.

Blue and gold golf umbrella with Mr. Peanut logo. 1980. $20-40.

Red and white golf umbrella with Heritage logo. 1991. $30-50.

Umbrella, red and white with Heritage logo. 1990. $25-35.

Plastic alarm clock
with the Heritage
logo. Mr. Peanut is
on the second hand.
1991. 2.5". $35-50.

Colorful umbrella with the Heritage logo. 1990. $80-100.

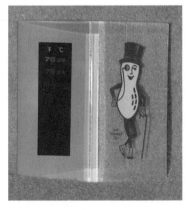

Lucite thermometer with Mr.
Peanut on front. 3.5". 1990.
$25-40.

Heritage logo wall clock in red and clear
plastic. 1991. $80-125.

Voice activated clock. 3.5". 1980s. $20-30.

Plastic Planters counter clock. Mr. Peanut logo in center. 1990. $20-25.

Plastic disposable Bic razor. 4.5". 1980s. $3-5.

Lucite digital clock. 2.5". 1988. $25-40.

Plastic tooth brushes with Mr. Peanut on ends. Newer style. Came in yellow, light blue and aqua. Different than the 1950 tooth brush. 1970s. $8-12 each.

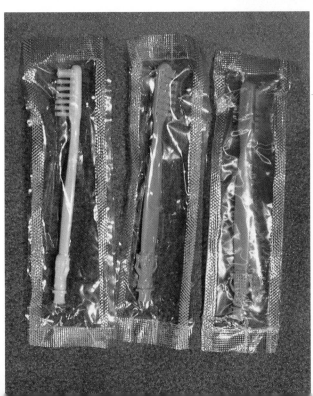

Mr. Peanut rubber volley ball "Kick 'n Throw". 6.5". 1970s. $20-30.

Basketball with Mr. Peanut logo by Wilson. 1989. $8-15.

Avon produced these peanut soaps in plastic peanut shell dish. The box shows Mr. Peanut. 1984. 7". $5-10.

Cooper baseball, white with black Mr. Peanut. 1979. $4-8.

Baseball with yellow, black and white Mr. Peanut. 1992. $3-6.

Blue and yellow blow up plastic beach ball with Mr. Peanut logo. 1974. $8-12.

Yellow tennis ball with Mr. Peanut. Made by Spalding. Another version has no marking on the ball but the container is marked Spalding. 1989. $9-15.

Football with Mr. Peanut logo by Wilson. There was also an earlier football made by Spalding. 1986. $10-15.

Golf ball. Ultra with Mr. Peanut logo. 1980s. $5-8.

Golf ball. DT-Titleist with Mr. Peanut logo. 1980s. $5-8.

Golf ball. Spalding with Mr. Peanut logo. 1980s. $5-8.

Heritage logo and reverse Heritage logo golf balls. 1990. $8-12 a sleeve.

Electric 4 car train set. 1971. $85-125.

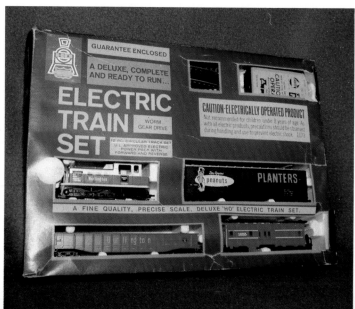

Battery operated 5 car train set. 1988. HO scale. $40-60.

Tyco HO scale train car. 1977.$15-30.

Lionel blue plastic train car. 1972. $30-45. There was also a train car in white plastic that is priceless, made by A. C. Gilbert. Only two known. 1960s. Watch for reproductions of the white one.

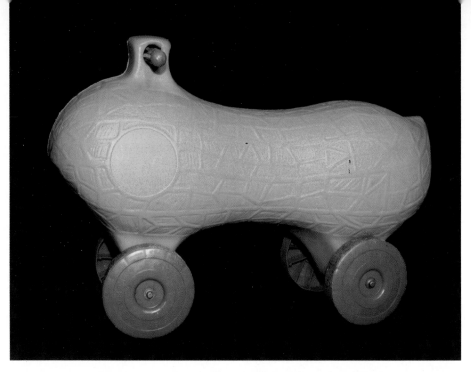

Child's plastic peanut-shaped riding toy. 1960s. $75-125.

Yellow plastic yo-yo with Mr. Peanut on front. 1976. $8-15.

Plastic yo-yo by Duncan with Mr. Peanut on front. 1980s. $15-25.

Saucer Tosser. Plastic, "frisbee" with paper label. 1970. $9-15.

Vinyl boat with motor and two oars. Yellow and blue. 1986. $50-100. Also (not shown), Round Rider inflatable inner tube. 1988. $20-40.

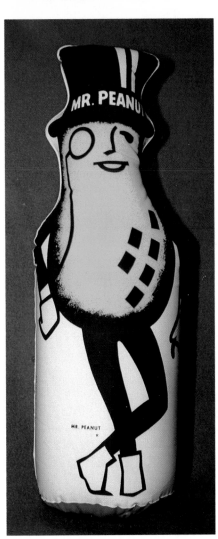

Hard white plastic frisbee with the Heritage logo. 1991. $15-25.

Nerf plastic frisbee, yellow with black Mr. Peanut. 1980s. $7-12. Also (not shown) orange hard plastic frisbee with Planters cheese balls written in blue. 1978. $10-20.

Vinyl punching bag. 26". 1980. $15-35. There is also a 48" version. $30-55.

Mr. Peanut costume, plastic top with cloth bottom, 1974. $25-45.

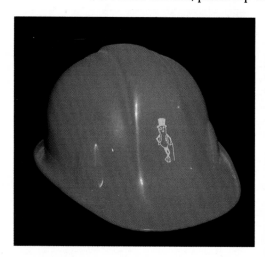

Plastic hard hat with Mr. Peanut emblem. Red, white or blue. 1990. $20-25.

"Tarco" plastic Mr. Peanut vending machine in the original box. 1978. $25-40.

Plastic youth cycling helmet with Mr. Peanut decals to stick on the helmet. 1993. $20-25.

Plastic Honey Roast nut dispenser. 1986. $12-20.

Canadian Mr. Peanut vendor. Mint in the box with the product. 1980s. $15-25.

Wind up walking toy. 1984. $8-20.

Plastic large pencil holder. 1968. $50-80.

Bendable rubber Mr. Peanut doll. 6".
1991. $5-8.

Plastic/cardboard Mr. Peanut barbell
balls puzzle. 1981. It came in red, blue,
or yellow. Price not available.

Plastic whizzer game with accessories.
1965. $50-70.

Plastic figural Mr. Peanut radio. 10.25".
1979. In box, $40-60.

Diamond shaped night light. Plugs into
wall socket. 1983. $12-20.

Lucite bank in a Planters, lightly salted, box form. Marked lightly salted on top. 5.5" x
2.5". 1990. $7-15.

Jukebox radio from Planters. 11" x 15".
1991. $80-125.

Plastic pencil sharpener. Originally sold
on bubble wrap card. 1983. $5-12.

Can shaped radio. 1978. 3.5". $30-50.

Figural eraser on bubble wrap card.
1983. $6-12.

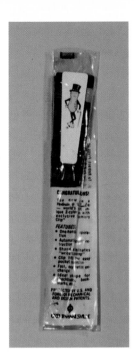

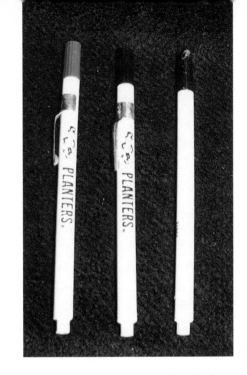

Ink pen that writes in blue or red ink, in original wrapping. 1980s. $5-10.

Ink pens write in black or blue. 1980s. $3-7 each.

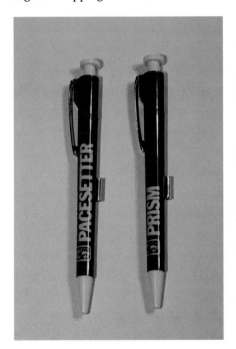

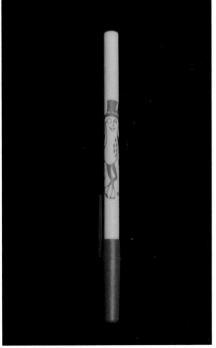

Ink pens. Pacesetter with Prism design, both have pull out profit chart. 1990. $4-7 each.

Bic blue and white stick pen. 1988. $2-4.

Lucite calendar cube from Military sales. 1984. 2.5". $15-25.

Lucite paperweight for Prism program for Planters. The Planters logo in etched in the center. 1990. $15-20.

Report book cover. 1980s. $5-10.

Plastic tape measure. 1.5". 1981. $4-8. Authenticity questionable.

Plastic envelope opener. 1993. $6-10.

Plastic envelope opener with the Heritage logo. 1991. $9-15.

Square tape measure from Planters 75th anniversary. 1906-1981. 1.7". $6-10.

White lighter with Mr. Peanut logo. 3". 1979. $10-15.

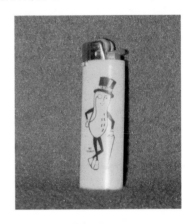

Plastic lighter with Mr. Peanut logo painted on front. 3.125". 1980s. $5-8.

Bic disposable lighter. 1980s. 3.125". $5-8.

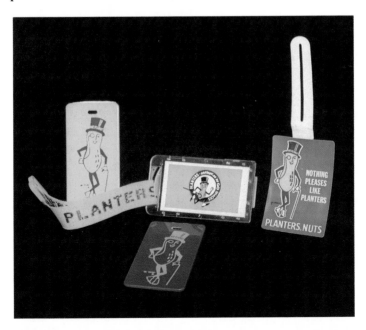

Vinyl and plastic luggage tags. 1980-1992. $8-15 each.

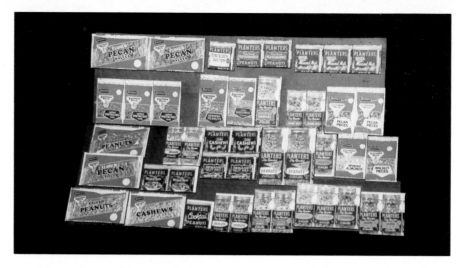

Small magnets shaped like Planters products designed to aid salesmen in product layouts. 0.25" to 2". 1970. $25-35 set.

Three leather belts with Planters logo. The belt on the left has Mr. Peanut on the buckle. 1960s. $30-50 each.

Brass buckle and leather belt with Mr. Peanut engraved in buckle. From Dinah Shore golf tournament. 1984. $20-30.

Plastic belt buckles with guns on the sides and Mr. Peanut logo in the bottom center. 4.25" x 1.75". 1960s. $6-10.

Vinyl lunch tote. 1980. 8.5" x 10.5". $15-25.

Plastic child's shoulder bag. 7" x 6.5". 1970s. $25-35.

Vinyl Cheez Balls cooler bag. 12.5". 1980. $15-25.

Vinyl Dry Roasted Peanuts bag. 10". 1976. $10-20.

525a/ Salesman's sample plastic peanut case. 1978. $150-200.

Vinyl seat cushion with handle. 1980s.
13.5". $10-15.

Insulated plastic picnic jug with
Planters Corn Chips logo. 1970s. $25-35.

Plastic license plate. Origin unknown. 1970s. $15-20.

"1992 Sales Jam Session" C.D. in a colorful plastic case. 1992. $10-20.

Plastic, full-figure Mr. Peanut cookie cutter. 1990. $6-15.

Hard plastic insulated ice chest. 1980s. $25-40.

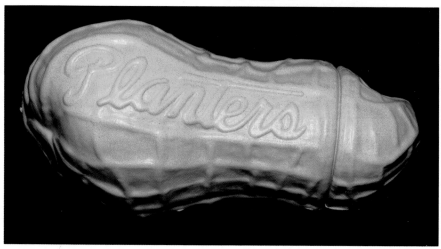

Plastic peanut. The end comes off to hold peanuts. 1978. 12.5". $4-8.

Metal

Metal advertising sign. 24" x 12.5". 1963. $50-75.

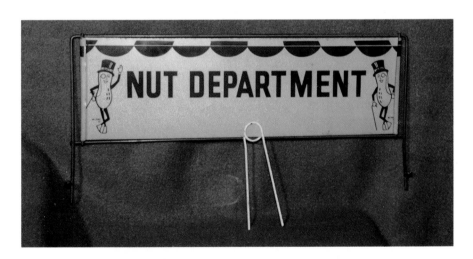

Metal header for peanut rack. 1964. $25-40.

Porcelain sign. 15.5" x
6.75". 1994. $16-25.

Planters metal counter
rack. Holds four boxes of
single-serve bags. 1988.
$15-25.

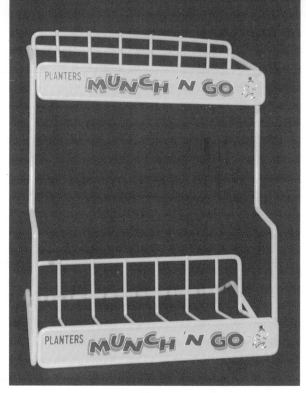

"Munch and Go" logo on metal counter
rack for Tabs nuts. 1992. $15-25.

10 ounce tin of Sweet 'n Crunchy Peanuts that is really a bank. 1980s. $7-12.

Yellow tin sign advertising the 5 cent bag of peanuts. 1970s. $50-75. Watch out for reproductions.

Metal Canadian hot drink vending machine. Approximately 5' x 3'. 1960s. Price not available.

Metal Canadian vending machine, in the four selection style. 1960s. Price not available.

12 ounce tin of Deluxe Mixed Nuts that is really a bank. 1980s. $7-12.

Canadian 10-cent vending machine. 1960s-70s. $350-450.

Planters product cans. 1960s. $30-50 each.

56 ounce product can with paper label. 1960s. $10-20.

Flat tin for Camp Fire Girls fund raiser. 12.5" x 4". 1970s. $15-25.

Two Planters nuts Girl Scout tins. 1960s-70s. $15-25 each.

4 oz. Cocktail Peanuts tin. 1960s. $10-15.

Red metal potato chip can. 1970s. $75-100.

One gallon of Peanut Oil in a gold tin can. 1989. $25-40.

One gallon of Planters Oil in gold stripped can. 1970. $30-40.

One gallon Planters Popcorn Oil. 1970s. $30-40.

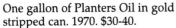

Five gallon blue round Planters Peanut Oil tin. 1970s. $50-60.

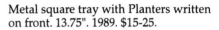

4" square tin with cut corners. Mr. Peanut on lid with nostalgic scenes on sides. 1994. $5-10. The metal trivet uses the same design motif, 8.375" x 6.5". 1995. Price not established.

Metal square tray with Planters written on front. 13.75". 1989. $15-25.

Metal ice cream scoop set in the original box. 1985. $20-35.

Five gallon Peanut Oil tin with gold stripe. 1970s. $30-50.

Two metal coasters/paperweight with "Heritage" logo in a wooden holder. 4". 1990. $35-50.

Wine coaster by Armetale. Pewter. Only 2000 made, numbered on the back. 1978. 6.5". $60-90.

Pewter Armetale plate by Wilton. Super Bowl 13. "Planters Snacks". 1978. 11.5". $40-70.

Brass coaster with leather insert. Engraved "Planters Life Saver, Nabisco Foods". 1994. $15-20.

"Bell Noggin" mug by Armetale. Pewter. 1978. 6.375". $20-30.

Mug by Armetale. Pewter. 1983. 5". $15-25.

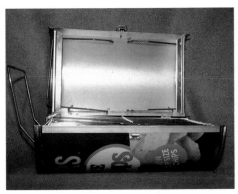

Metal barbecue grill from Planters in the shape of a corn chip can. Inside view. 14.5". 1972. $15-24.

Winter Olympics metal bowl and coaster set. 1980. Not shown is a matching coin. $40-75.

Souvenir spoon with small Mr. Peanut on top. 1978. $10-15.

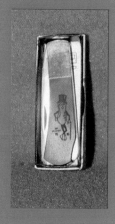

Dark brown and silver, one-blade knife with laser cut Mr. Peanut. 2.5". Unopened. 1990. $25-40.

Buck knife and leather case. Laser engraved. 1986. $70-100.

Blue knife with silver Mr.Peanut. This was also available in a larger version, and one with a jump ring and a different Mr. Peanut. It comes with a red or brown vinyl sleeve. 1989-90. $10-20.

Two-blade knife with Mr. Peanut attached on the front. 1990. $15-20.

Assortment of carton cutters. 1960-1994. $2-10.

Metal figural ashtrays. Left: ashtray marked 50th anniversary at back of feet. 1956. $25-35; Middle: plain gold wash Mr. Peanut ashtray. 1970s. $15-20; Right: chrome Mr. Peanut. 1992. $35-55.

Cocktail peanut tin lighter. 1960s. $40-50.

Souvenir ash tray from Atlantic City. Pot metal. 5.25" x 3.5". 1960. Price not available.

Metal belt buckle with embossed Mr. Peanut and Planters Peanuts. 1975. $15-25.

Cross pen and pencil set in box. Small Mr. Peanut on clip. No other design or writing. 1992. $50-90.

Metal magnet like the porcelain sign on page 42. 1993. 1.25" x 3". $3-5.

Metal alarm clock with red and yellow face. 1960. $65-100.

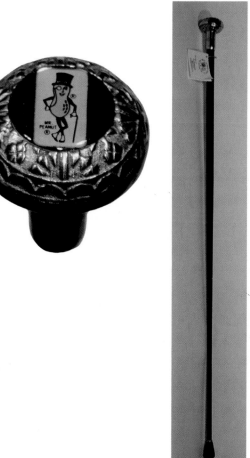

"Forklift" design tin license plate. 1987. $15-20.

Fiberglass, metal and plastic walking stick. 1994. Price not available.

Small metal waste paper can. 1968. $12-20.

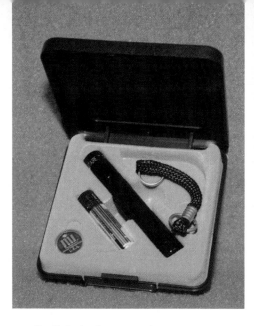

Penlight in the original case. 1990. 3.25".
$10-15.

Gotham electric baseball game with
Planters billboard in left field. 1960s.
$50-100.

Hollywood-styled light with Planters
logo on front panel. Plastic and metal.
Comes in black or red. 1991. $20-25.

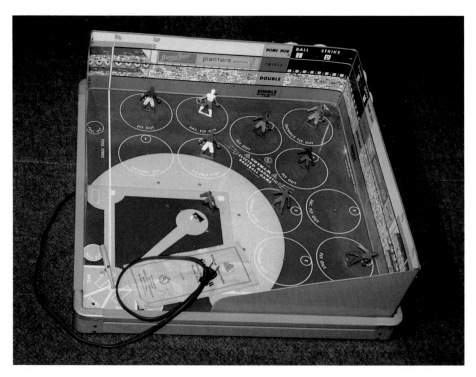

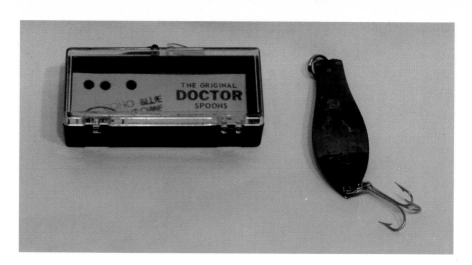

Fishing lure, the "Original Doctor Spoons". Coho blue and orange, #265. 1970s.
Authenticity questionable. $35-50.

Model A bank car with Planters logo.
This was an authorized toy. 1994. $15-
25.

Models of Yesteryear Planters truck.
1988. $25-35.

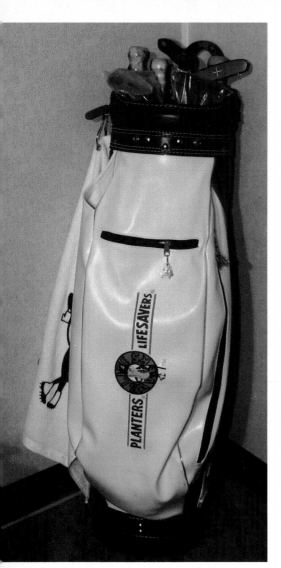

Putter with Mr. Peanut decal on handle and brass peanut as the club head. 1983. $125-150.

Plastic golf bag with Heritage logo. 1990. $300-400.

Calloway Hickory stick putter. U.S.A on shaft, Mr. Peanut medallion in bottom of club head. Little Parson #11 written on club. 1980s. $150-175.

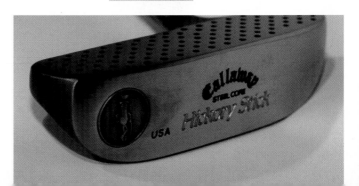

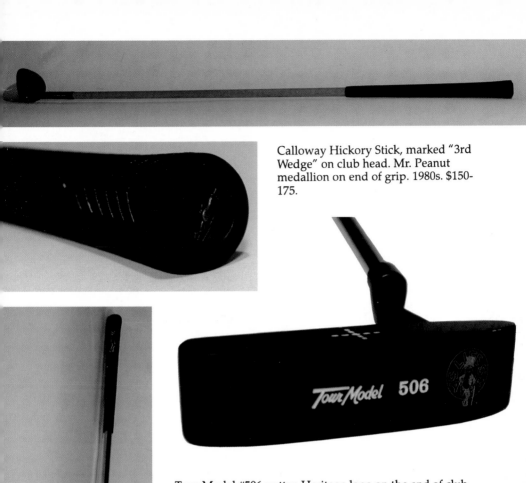

Calloway Hickory Stick, marked "3rd Wedge" on club head. Mr. Peanut medallion on end of grip. 1980s. $150-175.

Tour Model #506 putter. Heritage logo on the end of club.

Scooter curb cruiser with Mr. Peanut label on front post. 1988. 46" long. 1988. $60-90.

Glass

Salesman's sample leather carrying case with 24 ounce jar of peanuts. 1981. $30-50.

Salesman's sample kit. Very few made. 1979. $40-60.

Salesman's sample kit. 24 oz. decanter jar, nostalgic tin, and oval serving tray. 1982. $50-60 for the set. Tray only $20-30.

Five glass Planters jars. 1960s. $10-20 each.

Canadian peanut oil and popcorn oil in glass bottles. 1980s. $5-9.

Salesman's sample kit. 450 made. 1980. $30-50.

Glass pint of Planters popcorn oil. 1960s. $25-35.

Small fishbowl peanut jar with plastic fitted lid. Has brown design on one side. 1979. $35-50.

Glass miniature octagon peanut jar. "Made in Italy" embossed on bottom. "Planters 5 cent" embossed on front. 5.5". 1981. $50-80.

Anchor Hocking peanut jar with four products listed. White frosted and red. 1963. $60-80. Also (not shown) round jar with small paper label. 1965. $50-60.

Round apothecary jar with Heritage logo. 1990. $10-20.

Authentic Anchor Hocking round jar with four color silk-screen design. Note the wide white space above the T's. There are two reproduction versions. 7.625". 1966. $35-55.

Drinking 8 ounce glass that looks like the Cocktail Peanut tin. 1978. $8-12.

Glass beer mug by Anchor Hocking with "Fresh Roast", logo. 1991. $25-35.

Etched drinking glass with Mr. Peanut in rectangle. 1990. $8-12.

Pale blue glass with Planters, Lifesavers Nabisco, etched on front. 1994. $15-20.

Ceramic coffee cup by Nabisco. 1992.

Ceramic coffee cup with Heritage logo. 1990. $10-15.

Black ceramic coffee mug with gold Mr. Peanut. $10-15.

Glass cup and tile coaster. 1990. $20-30.

White ceramic cup and ashtray with raised Mr. Peanut design. 1990. $35-50.

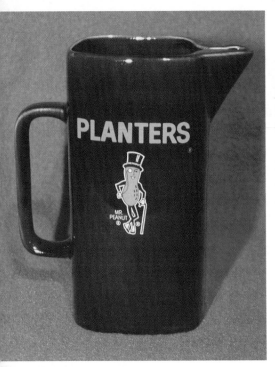

Thermochromic ceramic coffee mug. Design changes when hot liquid is added. 3.5". 1982. $12-20.

Small cobalt blue pitcher with Mr. Peanut logo painted on front. 1990. $75-100.

Glass bowl with blue Planters lettering on the side. Goes with the Planters and Lite beer football tray. 1984. $6-15.

Glass bowl with the etched Mr. Peanut inside rectangle. 1989. $12-20.

Ceramic full-figure Mr. Peanut cookie jar. 11.5". 1990. "Taiwan". $50-75. Authorized.

Terra Cotta nodder figurine with detachable cane. Matte finish. 6.5". 1962. $75-100.

Ceramic wall plaques. Only 300 authorized and made. 1982. $40-60. Prototypes: $100-150.

Ceramic full-figure Mr. Peanut spoon rest. 8.25". 1990. "Taiwan". 1992. $8-12. Authorized.

Ceramic full-figure utensil holder. 7.5". 1990. "Taiwan". $15-20. Authorized.

Ceramic full-figure Mr. Peanut magnets. 2.75". 1990. "Taiwan". $8-12. Authorized.

Ceramic full-figure Mr. Peanut napkin holder. 4" x 5". 1990. Taiwan. $10-15.

Ceramic full-figure Mr. Peanut salt and pepper set. 1990. Taiwan. $15-20.

Ceramic candy dish with Mr. Peanut on lid. Authentic. Price not available. 1992

Blue plaster Cocktail Peanut tin-shaped planter. 1970s. $20-30.

Tan plaster Cocktail Peanut planter. 1970s. $20-30

Snow globe from Planters, with the company name on a wooden base. 1988. $20-30.

White plaster Planters planter. 1970s. $20-30.

Plaster Dry Roasted Peanut planter. 1970s. $20-30.

Framed pub mirror. 14.5" x 17.5". 1980. $15-30.

Fabric and Clothing

Cloth duffle bag with yellow Mr. Peanut and Planters Peanuts written across the bottom.1983. $8-15.

Full size cotton apron. 1985. $8-15.

Cotton full size Gold Measure apron. 1991. $6-10.

Fresh roast rain poncho
in a pouch. 1991. 4" x 8".
$15-25.

Stadium blanket in vinyl holder. 1985.
$25-40.

Blue cloth tote bag with yellow Mr. Peanut and trim. 18". 1988. $10-20.

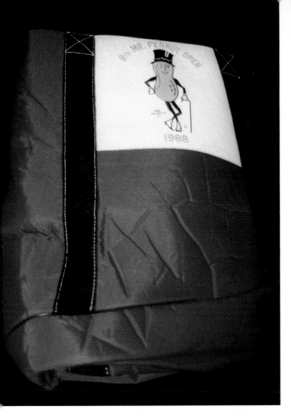

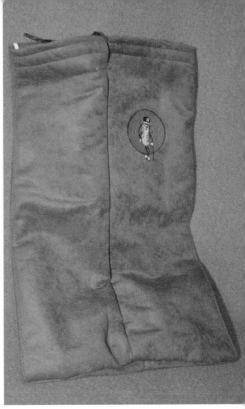

Nylon golf bag carrier with Mr. Peanut logo. 1988. $60-100.

Vinyl golf shoe bag with Heritage logo. 1990. $10-20.

Cloth 6-pack cooler bag. Yellow and blue. 1980s. $5-10.

Cloth cassette case. 1989.
$20-30.

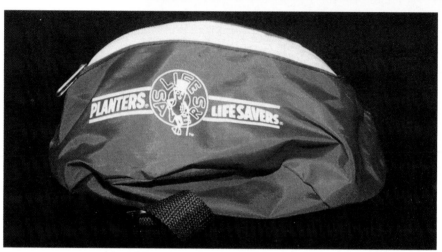

Blue and white nylon fanny pack with Heritage logo. 1990. $5-10.

Plastic fanny pack. Planters on top. Commemorates the Washington Capitals hockey team's 20th anniversary. 1993. $10-20.

White cotton Mr. Peanut shoe lace. 1984. $6-12 pair.

"Munch and Go" logo on a pair of cotton shoe laces. 1992. $3-5.

Cotton baseball cap with mesh back. Mr. Peanut's logo trimmed in gold. 1970s-80s. $4-7.

Wool knitted hat with Planters knitted into the front. 1977. $6-15. Other styles of knitted hats not shown.

Planters Nuts and Snacks cotton baseball cap. 1970s. $8-10.

Cotton baseball cap with Mr. Peanut logo in gold trim. 1970s-80s. $5-7.

Cotton baseball cap with mesh back. Planters with Mr. Peanut logo. 1970s. $5-7.

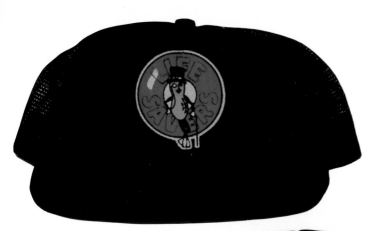

Cotton baseball cap with mesh back. Heritage logo on front. 1991. $8-12.

Cotton baseball cap with gold trim around Planters. 1980s. $5-10.

Cotton baseball cap with mesh back and Heritage logo on front. 1980s. $8-10.

Cotton baseball cap with the Heritage logo. 1991. $8-12.

Nylon Planters, Munch 'N Go baseball cap. 1990s. $4-5.

Felt Ocean City pennant with Mr. Peanut logo. 1960s. $30-45.

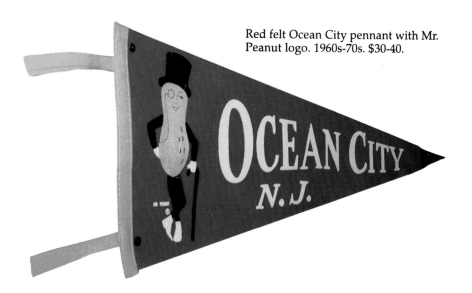

Red felt Ocean City pennant with Mr. Peanut logo. 1960s-70s. $30-40.

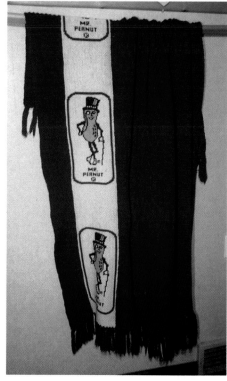

Black and white cotton afghan throw. 44" x 68". 1994. $50-70.

Blue knit afghan with front and back of Mr. Peanut. Also has matching sweater. 54" x 50". $30-50. 1990.

Cotton and nylon sleeping bag. Planters Salted Peanuts written across the front. 66" x 67". 1980. $60-100.

Cotton bath towel. It also came in hand towel size. 1980s. $8-20.

Cotton beach towel. 56" x 30". 1980s. $20-30.

Cotton terry cloth beach towel. 1970s. $50-75.

Cotton beach towel with Heritage logo.
54" x 36". $25-40. 1989.

Cotton golf towel. 1988. $10-20.

Bath towel 3-piece set with Mr. Peanut
and whale motif. 1984. $15-25 set.

Silk-like decals. They comes in stacks. 2". 1970s. $2-5 per stack.

Cotton patches of Mr. Peanut on peel off plastic. 1960s. $4-5 each.

Cotton Escape to the Tropics beach towel. 30" x 58". 1994. $15-25.

Embroidered Mr. Peanut clothing patch. 2.75" x 3.5". $2-5. Other similar patches were made, but are not shown.

Cotton Planters Safety Award patch. 3.5". 1980s. $5-10.

5 pound burlap bag from Suffolk Peanut store. 1989. $3-5.

3 pound burlap bag from Suffolk peanut store. 1989. $3-5.

Burlap tote bag. 1978. $8-12.

2 pound burlap bag. 1960s. $5-10.

Cloth stitched Mr. Peanut rag doll. 1970s. $5-10.

Mr. Peanut cloth, cotton stuffed doll. 20". 1978. $7-15.

5 pound burlap bag from Planters Peanuts. 1960s. $8-12. Other sizes up to 100 pound bags were made but are not shown.

Mr. Peanut cloth, cotton stuffed doll. 19". 1967. $10-20.

Plush small honey bear from Planters. 1980s. $15-25.

Mr. Peanut stuffed plush doll. 1992. $15-22.

Mr. Peanut stuffed doll with scarf. 1993. $15-25.

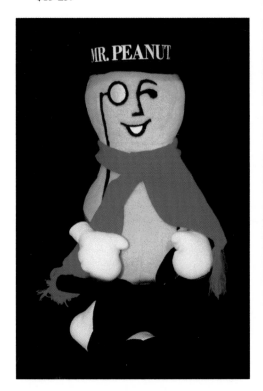

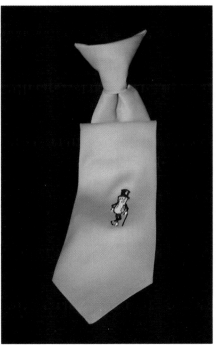

Silver, silk clip-on necktie with Mr. Peanut logo. 1980. $9-15.

Navy blue cotton necktie with Mr. Peanut logo. Also came in other colors. 1980. $9-15.

Cotton tee shirt with "Everybody loves a nut" imprinted on front. 1991. $7-12.

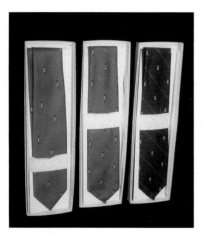

Cotton tee shirt from the Planters company. "Everybody loves a nut". 1993. $6-12.

Three silk Mr. Peanut ties. 1960s. $20-30.

Cotton tee shirt with Mr. Peanut
"Everybody loves a nut" silk screen.
1993. $5-8.

Cotton tee shirt with Mr.
Peanut hot air balloon
picture from the Balloon
Classic. 1993. $15-20.

Cotton sweat shirt with Heritage logo.
1991. $14-20.

Cotton sweat shirt with Planters "Come out of your shell and party" logo. 1989. $12-20.

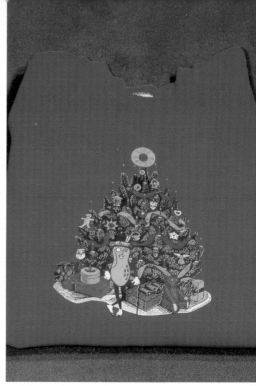

Red cotton Mr. Peanut Christmas sweat shirt. 1994. Authentic. $25-35.

Green cotton Mr. Peanut Christmas sweat shirt. 1994. Authentic. $25-35.

White cotton Christmas sweat shirt with Heritage logo. 1994. Authentic. $25-35.

Cotton oven mitt with "Gold Measure" logo. 1993. 14". $5-8.

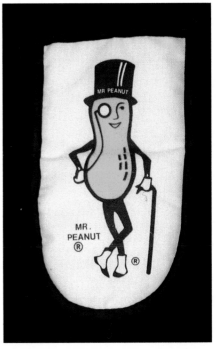

Cotton padded oven mitt. 1989. $7-12.

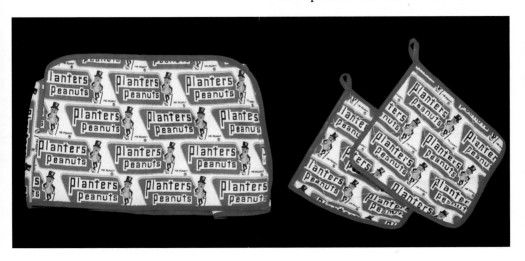

Cloth toaster cover and pot holders with Planters logo print. 1970s. $10-20.

"Nicole Miller" silk printed scarf, featuring Planters and Life Savers products. This fabric was also made into several different items. 1994. $60 for the scarf. Other items ranged up to $350.

Cotton sweat shirt with markers and instructions for coloring. 1980s. $15-30.

Cotton fabric with peanut bags in four colors. 1970. $5-9 a yard.

Set of four Mr. Peanut leather coasters. 1980s. $20-30.

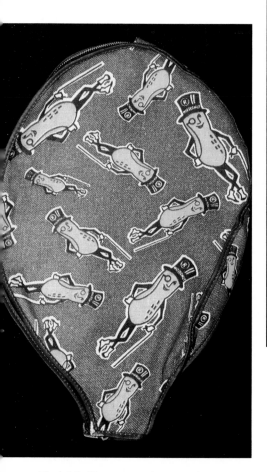

Cross stitch kit with Heritage logo. 1990.
5.25" x 5.5". $10-15.

Cloth Mr. Peanut tennis racquet cover.
1970s. $15-20.

Wood

Wooden Sweet 'N Crunchy churn. 1984. 5". Only 3,180 were made. $20-30.

Wooden large divided bowl. No marking of Planters or Mr. Peanut. 1980s. $10-15. Smaller wooden bowl with Planters logo. 1980s. $10-20.

Two sizes of wooden boxes for shipping. 5" x 8.5" and 13.5" x 7". 1970. $25-35.

Wooden and glass triple Mr. Peanut dispenser. 12.5". 1980. $25-45.

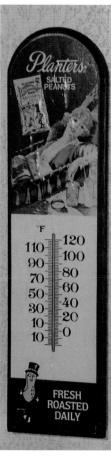

Wall thermometer. 17.5" x 4 1/2'. 1960s-70s. $40-75.

Wall thermometer. 1983. 23" x 5.5". $40-60.

Basket cooler with Mr. Peanut on lid. Foam insert inside. 1980s. $20-40.

Wooden and glass single Mr. Peanut dispenser. 8.75". 1980. $15-25.

Framed Mr. Peanut advertising sign. Wood covered in plastic. 1970s. $50-75.

Two wood and glass peanut dispensers. 13.5" tall. 1970s. $15-25.

Wall clock, horizontal with Roman numerals. 1993. $50-80.

Wooden Planters truck/bank. 6.75" x 4.75". 1981. $20-25.

Wooden truck with Mr. Peanut driving. 8". 1980s. $30-40. Also (not shown) wooden roadster. 1990. $40-60.

Evolution clock. Wooden case, glass front, gold pendulum. 1992. 12" x 21". $75-125.

Wooden rocking horse with Planters logo printed on back leg. 1988. 27" x 33". $50-75.

Wooden desk set with calculator, note pad and pen. 1980s. $30-50.

Dart board with 8 darts.
Inside and out. 16" x 20".
1985. $15-25.

Shuffleboard game with Heritage logo.
25" x 33. 1990. $150-200.

Winning Hand poker set in wooden box
with 4 colors of chips with Mr. Peanut
on each chip. Two decks of cards. 8" x
8.5". 1989. Price not available.

Cardboard Mr. Peanut and wooden bat.
35.5" bat. 1992. $15-20. Mr. Peanut 38".
$25-35.

Paper

Three bags of products from the 1960s. $6-12.

Cellophane 5 and 10 cent peanut wrappers. 1960s. $4-8.

Salesman's sample of Old Fashioned Jumbo Block candy bar. Upright Mr. Peanut in the corner. 1960s. $75-100.

Three boxes for the 5 cent peanut candy. 1960s. $20-30.

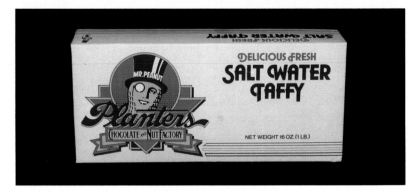

Salt Water Taffy, 16 ounce cardboard box. 1970s. $20-30.

Five boxes in a variety of sizes. 1960s. $20-40.

Seven boxes that held the single serve bags. 1970s. $10-20 each.

Paper peanut bags used by stores. 1960s-70s. $5-8 each.

Christmas holiday gift package. 1994. $5-10.

Boxed gift set. "Nut lovers". 1994. $10-20.

Cardboard popcorn container. 1980s. $3-5.

Three boxed gift set containing "Everybody loves a nut" napkins. $15-20.

Red/white/blue Mr. Peanut on paper shopping bag. 1970s. $10-20.

Cardboard Planters display from the 1980s. $30-45 without the products.

White paper shopping bag with Mr. Peanut on front. Compliments of Planters Peanut Store. 1970s. $10-20.

Three boxes of Quaker cereal with Planters offer. 1980s. $4-8 each.

Team flakes and Cheerios cereal in boxes with Planters offer. 1980s. $4-8 each.

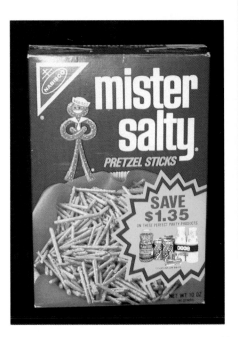

Mister Salty pretzels with Planters offer. 1980s. $4-8.

Scuff Kote shoe polish with Mr. Peanut advertising free prize inside. Prize was a balloon or a charm. Came in brown, black or white polish with at least two different graphics on the side. 1960s/ 1970s. With balloon or plastic charm: $35-50.

Various post cards from Atlantic City. 1960s-1970s. $3-15.

Various post cards from Atlantic City. Mid-1970s. $3-15.

Various post cards from Atlantic City. 1960s-1970s. $3-15.

Post card from Atlantic City Boardwalk.
1960s. $3-15.

Haggadah cook book from Planters.
1966. $5-10.

Various post cards. 1940s-1970s. $3-15.

Appliance Cooking for All Seasons cookbook. 1980s. $5-8.

The Fleischmann Treasury of Yeast Baking cook book from Planters. 1962. $5-10.

5 Great Cuisines cook book from Planters . 1980. $5-10.

Fleischmann's New Treasury of Yeast Baking. 1980s. $4-8.

Royal Recipes with a Flair cookbook. 1980s. $4-8.

New Royal Recipes with a Flair cookbook. 1980s. $4-8.

1993 *Home Baked Goodness* cookbook. 1993. $5-10.

Fleischmann's Bake-It-Easy Yeast Book. 1970s. $4-6.

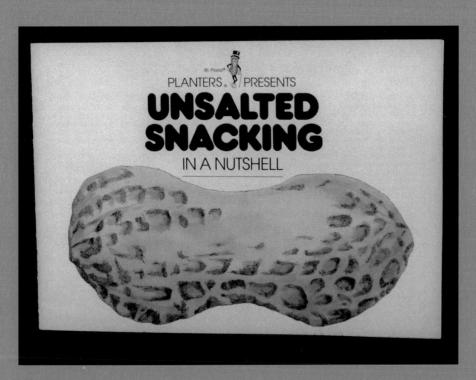

Unsalted Snacking cookbook from Planters. 1970s. $6-9.

Soup to Nuts cookbook from Planters. 1970s. $5-8.

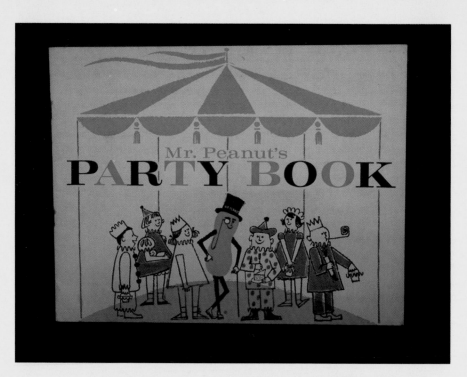

Mr. Peanut's Party Book cookbook. 1970s. $10-20.

Mr. Peanut's Guide to Entertaining. 1970s. $8-15.

Fun Days with Mr. Peanut. Story book. 1960s. $20-25.

The Personal Story of Mr. Peanut. 1960s. $10-20.

Paperback manual of Planters *Plant Rules.* 1960s. $10-20

The World of Mr. Peanut booklet. 1960s. $15-20.

Mr. Peanut's Guides. *Guide to Tennis*, 1969. *Guide to Nutrition*, 1970. *Guide to Ecology*, 1974. $4-7.

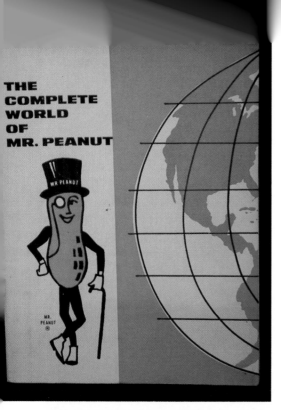

Mr. Peanut's Book of Magic. 1970s. $10-20.

The Complete World of Mr. Peanut. 1980s. $8-15.

Mr. Peanut's Guide to Physical Fitness and certificate. 1967. Booklet $5-8. Certificate $3-6.

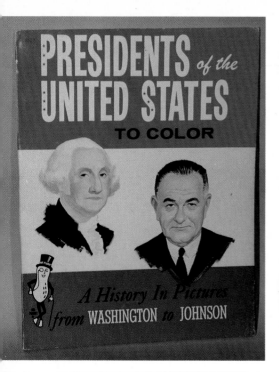

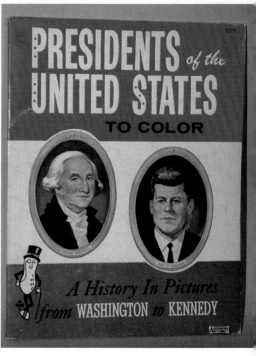

Presidents of the United States to Color. Washington to Johnson coloring book. 58 pages to color. 1965. $12-20.

Presidents of the United States to Color. Washington to Kennedy coloring book from Planters. 1963. $12-20.

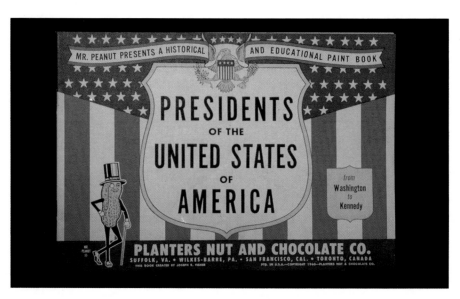

Presidents of the United States of America, Washington thru Kennedy, paint book. 1963. $15-25.

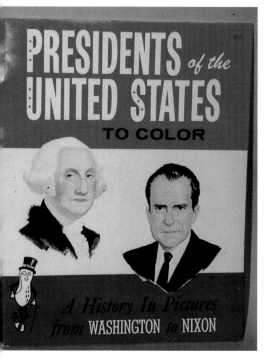

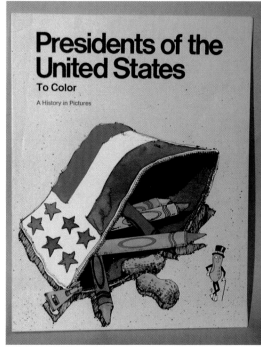

Presidents of the United States to Color. Washington to Nixon coloring book. 56 pages to color. 1969. $12-20.

50 States Coloring Book from Planters. 1968. $4-8.

Presidents of the United States to Color. 1970s. $4-8

Mr. Peanut at the finish line. Story book. 1970s. $10-20.

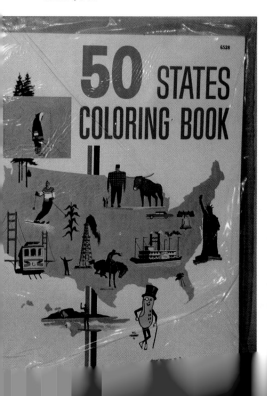

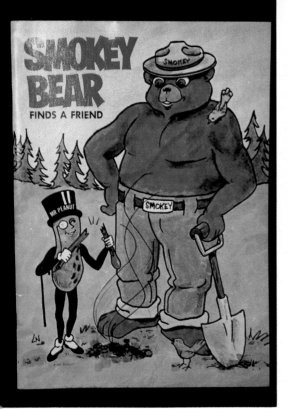

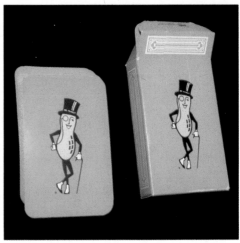

Plastic-coated Canadian playing cards with Mr. Peanut logo on fronts. 1980s. $20-30.

America: An Ecology Coloring Book from Planters. 1972. $4-8.

Smokey Bear Finds a Friend, story book. 1971. $8-15.

Double set of playing cards with Mr. Peanut logo on fronts. 1970s. $30-40.

Deck of cards with Mr. Peanut logo.
1980s. $6-10.

Double deck of playing cards in case.
One has Heritage logo and one has Mr.
Peanut logo. 1990. $12-20.

Roll of paper labels with hot air balloon
image. 1993. $10-15.

Roll of labels with Planters logo with a
spaces for net weight and price. 1970s.
$10-15.

Deck of playing cards with the Munch
'N Go logo. 1994. $3-5.

Presenting "Yellow", puzzle from
Hallmark/Springbrook. 20" x 20". 1992.
$10-20.

Between Meals Candy Bar
Puzzle by Hallmark/
Springbrook. 20" x 20". 1977.
$15-25.

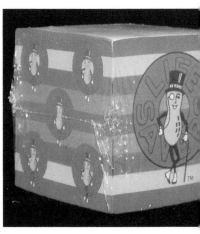

Colorful paper memo cube
with Heritage logo. 1990. 3".
$15-25.

Old country store puzzle from Hall-
mark/Springbrook. Mr. Peanut jar by
register. 500 pieces. 20.25" x 20.25".
1980s. $15-20.

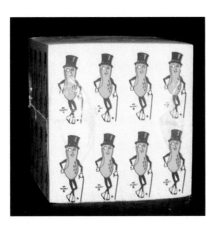

Square scratch paper memo cube. 3.75".
1990. $8-15.

Paper memo cube with Planters snacks
imprinted on cube. 1990s. 3.5". $7-15.

Mr. Peanut puzzle with all Planters
products, by Hallmark/Springbrook.
18" x 23.5". 1987. $20-30.

Paper note pad with Heritage logo.
1991. $5-7.

Paper note pad with the Cocktail Peanuts logo, came in two sizes. 1970s. $12-20.

Hot air balloon stickers featuring the Mr. Peanut hot air balloon. 1993. $2-4.

Three foil stickers: Christmas, Thanksgiving and St. Patrick's day. 1960s. $4-8 each.

Wall clock that was part of a large display. Orange, yellow and blue. 12.75" x 17.25". 1980. $20-30. Whole display $50-75.

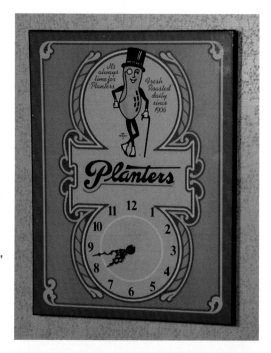

Paper cocktail napkins. 1993. $1.

Package of paper cocktail napkins. 1983.
$3-7.

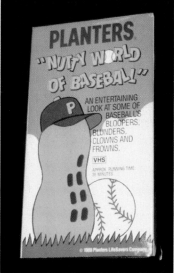

1988 video tape of the
"Nutty World of Baseball."
$8-15.

Display container made of
cardboard and plastic. 13" x
11.5". 1968. $15-30.

Cardboard blotter coaster. Mr. Peanut on front and "Americas Number 1 Selling Nut" on back. 4 ". 1993. $5-7.

Paper fold out ads. The two outside ads "Do you know?" $10-20. The center ad Nostalgia, 1980s. $5-10.

New style stand up cardboard Mr. Peanut. 1989. 48". $10-20. Also shown "out" sticker from an "in & out" set for store glass doors. $8-$15.

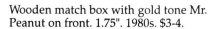

Book of matches advertising Planter dry roasted peanuts. 1970s. $20-25.

Wooden match box with gold tone Mr. Peanut on front. 1.75". 1980s. $3-4.

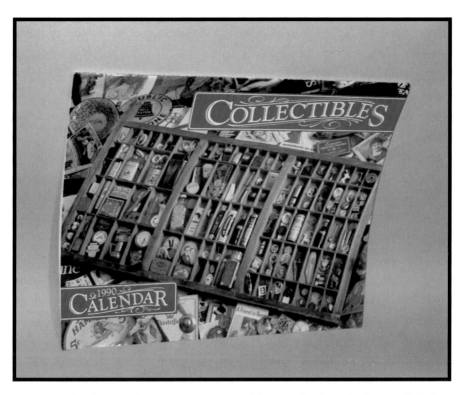

1990 calendar that shows a Mr. Peanut red figure whistle, in background. $5-8.

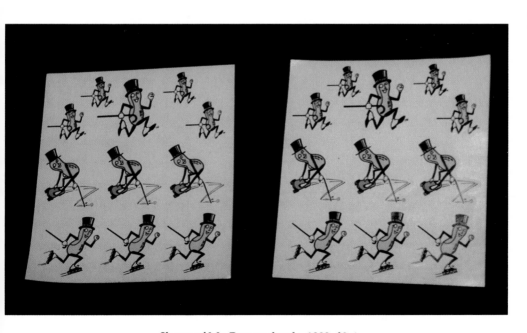

Sheets of Mr. Peanut decals. 1992. $2-4.

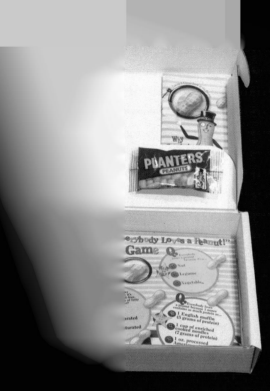

White cardboard box that holds the Peanut quiz game with sound effects. 9" x 12.5". 1993. $15-25.

Our hit parade poster. 1970s. $100-150.

"OUR HIT PARADE"

Jewelry

Gold tone cuff links with figure of Mr. Peanut inside oval. 1962. $45-75. Also (not shown) figural Silvertone Mr. Peanut cuff links with one raised hand. 1950s. $100-150.

Various pin back pins. 1976-1993. 2" to 4". $3-10.

Various metal pin back pins. 1976-84. $6-8 each.

Gold tone and blue enamel 75th anniversary pin. 1981. $15-20.

Enamel Mr. Peanut tie pin. 1970s. $10-15.

Full figure Safety award pin from the company. 1970s. $25-40.

Plastic yellow/blue tie tack. 1". 1980s. $3-6.

Double flag enamel pin with Mr. Peanut. 1". 1970s. $10-20.

Enamel Mr. Peanut on white background, pin back. 1". 1994. $10-15.

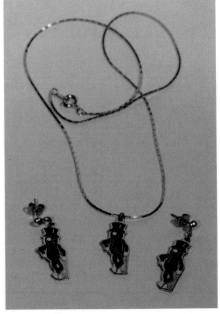

Gold tone necklace and earrings with black Mr. Peanut. 1979. $10-20 set.

Gold tone peanut necklace. 1980. Not authorized. $5-8.

Gold tone figural Mr. Peanut necklace. 1.25". 1984. $15-25.

Kentucky Derby hot air balloon, enamel pin backs. 1986-1988. $15-25.

Pink iridescent plastic bracelet with Mr. Peanut printed on band. 1982. $20-30.

Two Jaycees pins. 1980s. 1 ". $25-30 each.

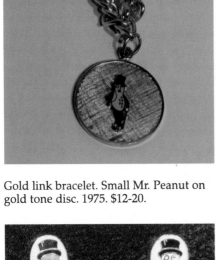

Gold link bracelet. Small Mr. Peanut on gold tone disc. 1975. $12-20.

Special Shape Rodeo, New Mexico hot air balloon pin.   1989. $30-40.

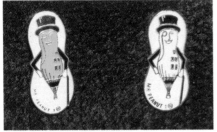

Two hot air balloons, a yellow Mr. Peanut and a green Mr. Peanut. 1980s. $25-30.

Three metal Lions Club pins. Full figure Mr. Peanut. 1985-87. $60-85 each.

Set of five hot air balloon pins. 1988-1992. $6-10 each.

Hot air balloon pin. 1993. $25-40.

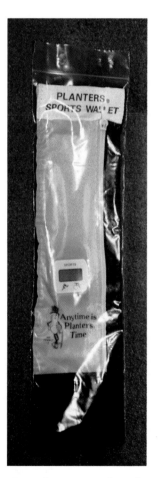

Yellow face Mr. Peanut watch with blue plastic strap. 1966. $45-60.

Blue face digital Mr. Peanut watch with blue strap. 1974. $40-60.

Digital sports watch with velcro closure. 1989. $10-20.

Lady's gold watch with gold stretch band. Mr. Peanut is on the dial. 1988. $35-50.

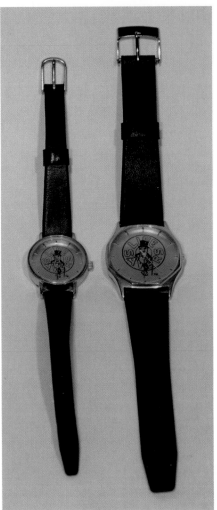

Lady's and man's gold face watches with black Heritage logo. 1990. $60-90 each.

Man's watch with leather band. White dial with yellow/black/white Mr. Peanut. By Adec in original case. 1988. $40-50.

Brass Munch 'N Go key chain. 1991. $4-7.

Man's and lady's Europa quartz watches with Roman numerals on the bezel. 1993. $40-50.

Mr. Peanut's 75th Birthday, watch with plastic strap. 1991. $25-35.

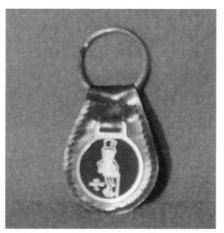

Full figure rubber Mr. Peanut key chain. 1989. $5-8.

Leather key chain with a metal insert of Mr. Peanut. 2.5". 1977. $8-15.

Plastic key chain with Mr. Peanut logo printed on front. 5". 1970s-80s. $8-12. Authenticity questionable.

Plastic #1 key chain. 1980s. $5-8.

Munch 'N Go brass key chain. 2.25". 1994. $2-5.

Plastic mini-flashlight with pull-apart key chain. 1950s. $6-10.

75th Birthday

75th birthday items on display. 1991.

Glass jar in original box, celebrating the 75th Birthday of Mr. Peanut. 1991. $10-20.

Three commemorative tin Canadian peanut containers from Mr. Peanut's 75th Birthday. 1991. $35-50 set.

Tin 75th birthday mixed nut container. 1991. $2-4.

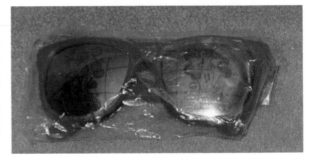

Plastic 75th Birthday sunglasses. 1991. $10-20.

Mr. Peanut advertising his 75th birthday. 1991. $5-10.

Cardboard and plastic display-held the round tins commemorating Mr. Peanut's 75th birthday. 1991. $25-35 each.

Mr. Peanut's 75th Birthday. Set of four cork coasters. 1991. $3-5.

Three Planters cheese snack cardboard rounds and plastic lids. 75th Birthday logo cork coasters on lid. 1991. $2-4.

Plastic 75th Birthday
edition Mr. Peanut bank.
1991. $10-15.

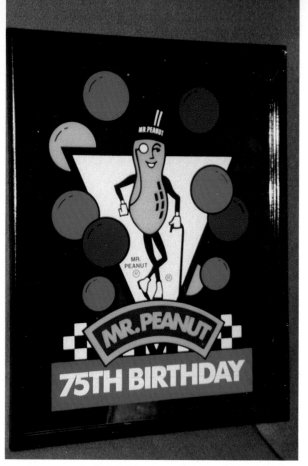

Mr. Peanut 75th Birthday wall mirror. 1991. $75-110.

Glass shot glass with the Mr. Peanut
75th Birthday logo. 1991. $10-18.

Cotton bath towel commemorating Mr.
Peanut's 75th Birthday. 1991. $25-40.

Beer glass with the 75th birthday logo.
1991. $15-25.

Peanut jar with a red fired on 75th
Birthday logo. 1991. Authorized. Price
not available.

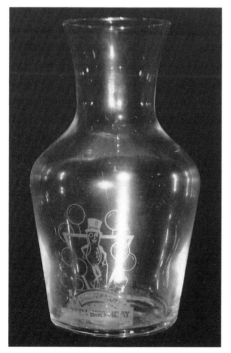

Wine carafe with the 75th Birthday logo.
1991. $20-35.

Apothecary square jar with the 75th
birthday logo. 1991. $25-50. Inside are
birthday balloons of various colors. $2-4.

Mr. Peanut 75th Birthday enamel pin. 1991. $30-40.

Mr. Peanut wall clock from the 75th Birthday. 1991. $75-125.

Gold plated money clip from Mr. Peanut's 75th Birthday. 1991. $10-20.

Insulated cooler bag from 75th Birthday. 1991. $15-20.

Cotton tee shirt commemorating Mr. Peanut's 75th Birthday. 1991. $15-20.

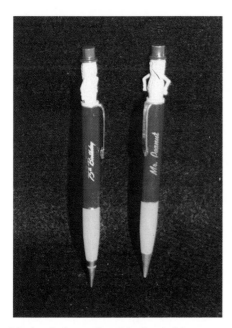

Mechanical pencils with plastic Mr. Peanut on top. Left: 75th Birthday version, $8-15. Right, regular version, $4-8.

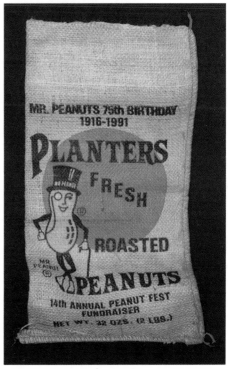

Burlap peanut bag with Mr. Peanut's 75th Birthday logo. 1991. 2 pound size. $8-12.

Two foam cup holders advertising Mr. Peanut's 75th Birthday. 1991. $5-9.

Mr. Peanut's 75th Birthday plastic visor. Questionable authenticity. 1991. $5-8.

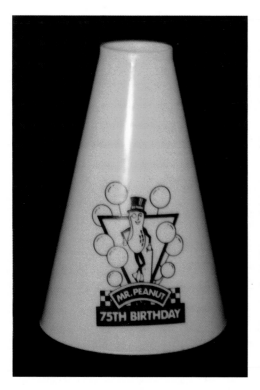

Plastic megaphone from the 75th birthday. 1991. Questionable authenticity. $4-8.

Plastic frisbee rings from Mr. Peanut's 75th Birthday. 1991. Questionable authenticity. $3-5.

Silver coin commemorating Mr. Peanut's 75th birthday. 1991. Only 2,120 made. Number on coin edge must match the certificate in the box. Price not determined.

Mr. Peanut's 75th birthday key chain. 1991. $10-20.

Plastic frisbee commemorating Mr. Peanut's 75th birthday. 1991. $10-20.

Pat Bradley

White plastic Pat Bradley logo cup. 1990. $3-5.

Pat Bradley stool and cooler combination. 1990. $60-100.

Paper poster from the Pat Bradley International Golf Tournament. 1988. $40-50.

Cardboard parking lot sign from the Pat Bradley golf tournament. Mr. Peanut logo in the corner. 24" x 18". 1990s. $10-15.

Caddie Jacket from Pat Bradley golf tournament. 1990. $25-30.

Plastic Pat Bradley can holder 1990. $5-10. Clear plastic glass. 1990. $2-4.

Pat Bradley green foldable canvas chair with carrying case. 1990. $50-80.

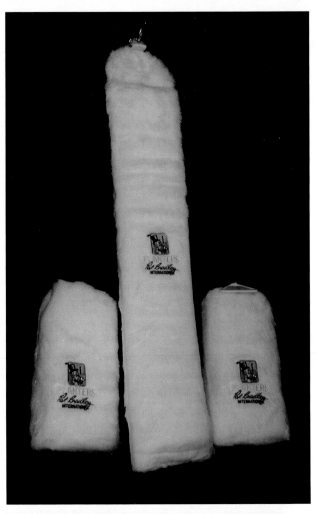

Glass with etched golfing Mr. Peanut from Pat Bradley International Tournament. 1990. $10-15.

Pat Bradley golf bag strap cover and golf club head cover. 1990. $25-40 each.

Pat Bradley golf terry cloth towel. 1990. $10-15.

Pat Bradley locker bag. 1990. $45-80.

Cotton shirt with Mr. Peanut Pat Bradley logo. 1990. $10-15.

Golfing Mr. Peanut cotton white and blue or blue stripe tube socks. 1989. $6-12 pair.

Cotton "Pat Bradley" golf cap, from the Pat Bradley International Golf Tournament. 1990s. $8-10.

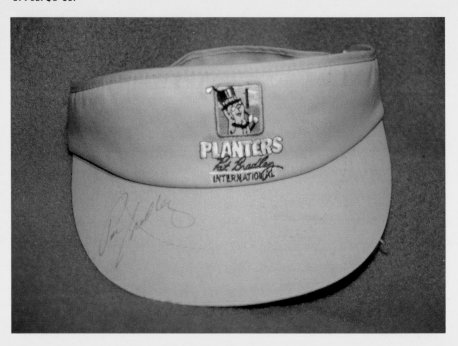

Autographed cloth visor from Pat Bradley golf tournament. 1990. $50-75.

Cotton "Pat Bradley" golf cap, from Pat Bradley International Golf Tournament. 1990s. $8-10.

Nylon "Pat Bradley" golf cap. From the Pat Bradley International Golf Tournament. 1990. $8-10.

Cotton "Pat Bradley" golf cap, from the Pat Bradley International Golf Tournament. 1990s. $8-10.

Nascar

Plastic flag from Nascar racing team. 1992. $12-20.

Cardboard
Planters and
Keystone Beer,
header card. 1993.
$10-15.

Nascar go-cart with authentic Keystone Planters logo. 1993. Price not available.

Cardboard header for Planters rack. 1992-93. $10-15.

Race car two-pack carton of nuts. 1992. $5-10.

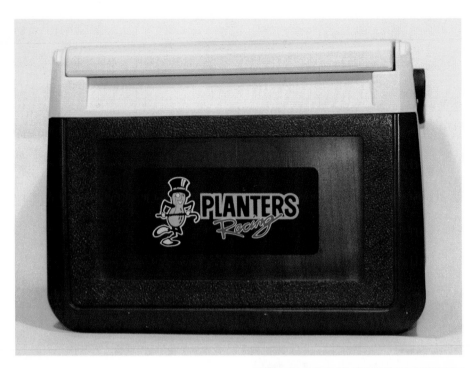

Plastic cooler, Nascar Racing sponsored by Planters. 1993. $20-30.

Plastic Keystone Planters car sealed in bottom of the mug. 1993. $40-60.

"The Nuttiest Moments in Stock Car Racing" video, by National Foods. 1992. $10-15.

Nascar cardboard trading cards, sponsored by Planters. 1993. $2-3 each.

Cardboard Nascar racing trade card. 1992. $2-3.

Cardboard Nascar racing trade card. 1992. $2-3.

Cardboard Nascar racing trade card. 1992. $2-3.

Die cut stand up Banquet trading card. Planters driver. 3". 1991. $35-50.

Nascar cardboard trading cards, sponsored by Planters. 1993. $2-3 each.

Moly Black gold/Planters card 1991. $10-15. Moly Black racing car. 1991. 1/64 scale. $10-20.

Planters/Roush toy racing car with card. 1/64 scale. 1993. $15-25.

Roush Planters toy racing car. 1/64 scale. 1992-93. $5-10.

Banquet Foods/Planters die cast Nascar. 1/64 scale. 1991. $12-15.

Roush/Planters toy racing car. 1/64 scale. 1992-93. $5-10.

Roush toy racing car in original box. 1/43 scale. 1992-93. $5-9.

3 pack of toy cars with the Roush racing car in original package. 1/64 scale. 1992—93. $12-18.

Moly Black Gold 1/43 scale toy car from Planters. 1991. $15-20.

Keystone Beer / Planters racing car in original box. 1/64. 1993. $12-20.

Roush toy racing car with driving trade card, in original box. 1/64 scale. 1993. $15-25.

Die cast Roush/Planters toy racing car. 1/24 scale. 1992. $25-35.

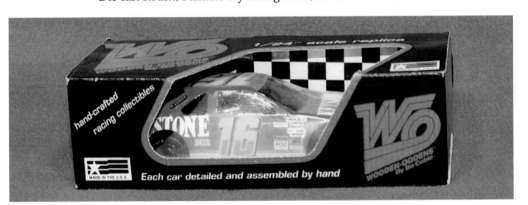

Wooden Keystone racing car in original box. 1/24 scale. 1993. Scripture printed inside the lid of the box. $55-65.

Toy transporter, Roush/Planters. 1/64 scale. 1992. $25-35.

Planters yellow nascar racing team hat with Mr. Peanut logo. 1993. $7-12.

Nascar racing team white cotton hat. 1992. $9-15.

Planters Nascar racing team black hat. 1993. $7-12.

Cotton tee shirt from Planters peanuts, with the racing logo. 1993. $5-9.

Nascar racing team dark blue acrylic sweater. 1992. $40-50.

Racing team jacket. Navy blue, poplin material with large logo on back also. 1992. $75-100.

Cotton tee shirt with a Nascar logo, for Planters sponsored Nascar racing. 1993. $5-9.

Nascar racing team jacket. Navy blue with yellow trim. 1993. $85-110.

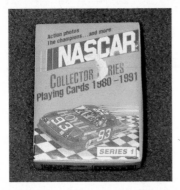

Nascar facts playing cards. Not Planters. 1980s. $2-5.

Keystone/Planters mounted trade cards. 1993. Not authentic. $4-6 each.

After market Nascar card with knife. 1992. $10-15.